樋口大輔

No one can always do what is right. I think about different ways of doing things, but I end up just facing things head-on. That's just the way I am. It's natural for people to have different opinions. You clash with people, express your opinions and try to understand those of others. This is how relationships are built. How sad it would be if we didn't have this process of working things out. It would be like existing all by yourself on this planet of ours.

- Daisuke Higuchi

Daisuke Higuchi's manga career began in 1992 when the artist was honored with third prize in the 43rd Osamu Tezuka Award. In that same year, Higuchi debuted as creator of a romantic action story titled ***Itaru***. In 1998, ***Weekly Shonen Jump*** began serializing ***Whistle!*** Higuchi's realistic soccer manga became an instant hit with readers and eventually inspired an anime series, debuting on Japanese TV in May of 2002.

WHISTLE!
VOL. 11: RUN

The SHONEN JUMP Manga Edition

STORY AND ART BY
DAISUKE HIGUCHI

English Adaptation/Drew Williams
Translation/Naomi Kokubo
Touch-up Art & Lettering/Jim Keefe
Cover, Graphics & Layout/Sean Lee
Editor/Andy Nakatani

Managing Editor/Elizabeth Kawasaki
Director of Production/Noboru Watanabe
Vice President of Publishing/Alvin Lu
Vice President & Editor in Chief/Yumi Hoashi
Sr. Director of Acquisitions/Rika Inouye
Vice President of Sales & Marketing/Liza Coppola
Publisher/Hyoe Narita

Printed in the U.S.A.

Published by VIZ Media, LLC
P.O. Box 77010
San Francisco, CA 94107

SHONEN JUMP Manga Edition
10 9 8 7 6 5 4 3 2 1
First printing, May 2006

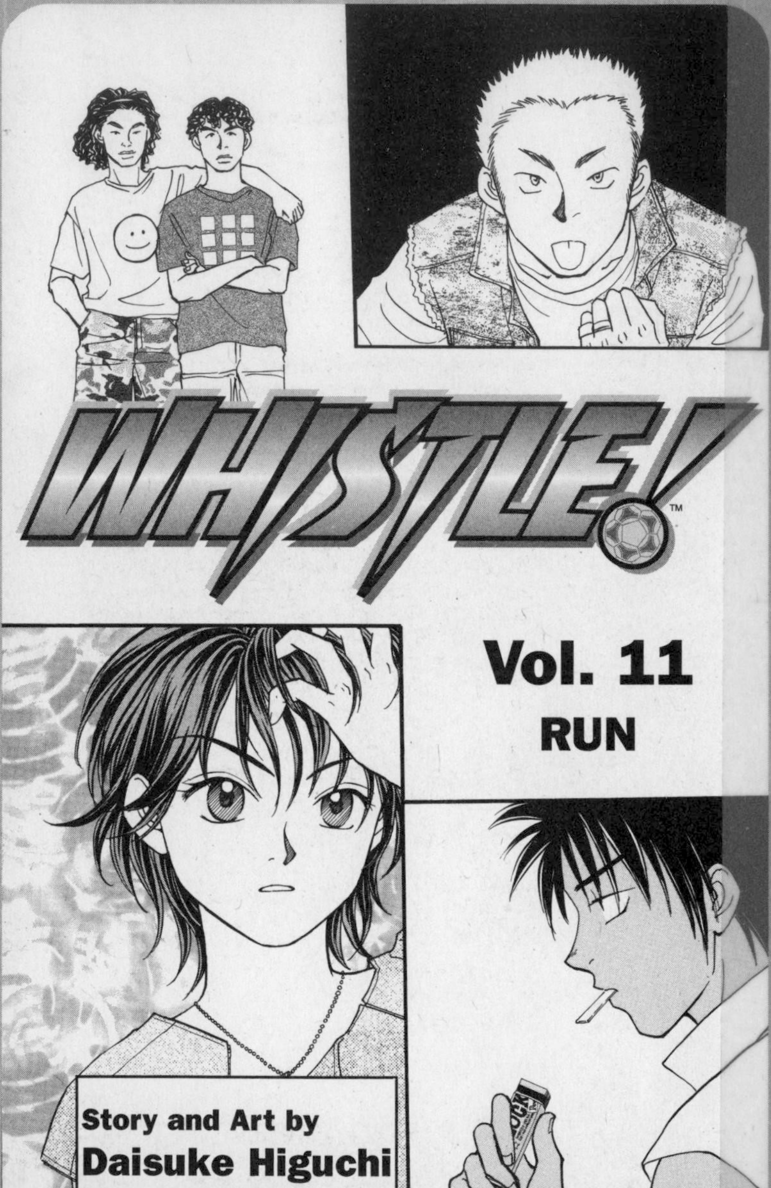

WHISTLE!™

Vol. 11
RUN

Story and Art by
Daisuke Higuchi

CHARACTERS

SHŌ
KAZAMATSURI

- JOSUI JUNIOR HIGH
SOCCER TEAM
FORWARD

KŌ
KAZAMATSURI

YŪKO
KATORI

TATSUYA
MIZUNO

- JOSUI JUNIOR HIGH
SOCCER TEAM
MIDFIELDER

SOUJŪ MATSUSHITA

FORMER JAPAN LEAGUE PLAYER

JOSUI JUNIOR HIGH COACH

TSUBASA SHIINA

HIBA JUNIOR HIGH SOCCER TEAM

CENTER BACK

SHIGEKI SATŌ

JOSUI JUNIOR HIGH SOCCER TEAM

FORWARD

STORY

To realize his dream, Shō Kazamatsuri, a bench warmer at soccer powerhouse Musashinomori, transferred to Josui Junior High so he could play the game he loves.

Josui's soccer team was a joke until Soujū Matsushita, a former Japan League player, took on the coaching duties. Under Matsushita's guidance, the team has become a force to be reckoned with. In the third game of the district primary tournament, they defeated Rakuyō Junior High after a fierce battle in the rain.

An unseeded team, Hiba Junior High, is Josui's final opponent in the tournament. Led by a brilliant center back, Tsubasa Shiina, Hiba quickly established dominance in the game. Then Shō broke through the defense, and Tsubasa gave chase...

WHISTLE!™

Vol. 11
RUN

STAGE.90
The Offense of Hiba Junior High
7

STAGE.91
Tsubasa Is on Fire
25

STAGE.92
First Score
46

STAGE.93
Off in the Distance
69

STAGE.94
The Tying Goal
91

STAGE.95
Decision
113

STAGE.96
I'm Going to Win
135

STAGE.97
RUN
155

STAGE.98
The Winning Goal
177

STAGE.90 The Offense of Hiba Junior High

OOM

NO. 9 SHOOTS !!
FO

BUT...
...IT'S HEADED STRAIGHT FOR THE KEEPER!
HIBA
SWAP
SHWOOM
!

JUMPED?
QUICK... FOR A FAT DUDE!
ZUPP
JOOP
PHEW!
FUMP

OOPS!
YOU DROPPED THE BALL!
WHAT ARE YOU "PHEWING" ABOUT?
ROLL ROLL
CLOSE ONE.
WHAT WAS THAT ABOUT? HOW DID I MISJUDGE THAT SHOT?
GRIP
GOOD STOP.
YOU THINK SO? THAT SHOT SEEMED LIKE A GIFT TO ME.
TSU-BASA.
YEAH.
TOSS

HE BROKE THROUGH.
FIRST TIME *THAT'S* HAPPENED.
HE TOOK IT INTO THE GOAL BOX.
THAT KID...
HE'S PRETTY GOOD, BUT...
FWIP
HIBA

!
SHOOOM
THE CENTER BACK...IS *DRIBBLING* ?!
ISN'T HE THE SWEEPER?
NO. 4 KICKS IT BACK.
THUP

DASH
!
AHH!
DASH

BOTH OF HIBA'S WINGS ARE MAKING A RUN FOR THE GOAL !!
OOM
TOSUI
TOSUI
WHO WILL GET THE PASS?
THOOM
HIDEOMI, MARK NO. 6!

WHILE NO. 4 DISTRACTED JOSUI, HIBA'S OFFENSE MADE THEIR MOVE.
THEY'RE QUICK!
SHO
FUMP

SHOOM
BIP
ANOTHER ATTACKER IS TRAILING!!
FWAP
NICE SAVE BY THE KEEPER.
YIKES
SHIVER
TUMP
HE SHOOTS !!
CORNER KICK FOR HIBA.
FOCUS!

JOSUI IS IN A PINCH.
WILL HIBA MAKE THE MOST OF THIS OPPORTUNITY?
JOSUI
HIBA
I BET THEY'LL USE A TALLER PLAYER.
YES.
MAKE SURE YOU FIND YOUR MARKS!
THERE HE IS!
SWIVEL SWIVEL
WHY IS HE OVER THERE?

TWEE
THERE'S THE WHISTLE!!

DO-O-OMMM

NEAR SIDE?
OR FAR SIDE?
WHAT THE...?
!?
DID HE SHANK IT?
WHO'S GETTING THE KICK?
VOOOSH

NO. 4
IS OPEN!
HIBA

OH NO...
THEY SNOOKERED JOSUI!
NO WAY! NOT FROM THAT SPOT!
THOOO
VOLLEY SHOT!!

!
SWAAPP

STAGE.91 Tsubasa Is on Fire

SHAPPP

WHUMP
OOF!
THUMP

SKR RR
SHŌ!
NO! NOT YET!

SKRR
FUMP
THE BALL IS STILL...
FOOOOOOM
... ALIVE!
TUMP

CLASH
HIBA
SCOOP
HIBA
BOMP
LUNGE

DAICHI!
NO!
NO TIME TO TURN AROUND.
UP
FW
WHOOSH

WHAT?!
A HAND-STAND ?!
WHOA! SERIOUSLY ?!
HIGUITA-ESQUE?
BOOOOM
WHAT ...
...AN ACROBATIC CLEARANCE!
DUDE! THAT'S MY TRADE-MARK!

SHOOM
FOOOMP
GO! MASATO!
OH NO! GET BACK!!
HIBA

WHOOSH
TOSUI
THEY'RE COUNTERING!
THE SITUATION QUICKLY REVERSES, AND NOW HIBA IS IN A PINCH!
NOW IT'S OUR TURN!

DASH
AHH! THE DEFENSE CAN'T CATCH UP!!
VOOOSH
IT'S ONE-ON-ONE WITH THE KEEPER!

IT'S MINE!
MASATO !!
DON'T GET CARRIED AWAY.
HUH?
WHOOSH
SHOOM

FWAM

THUP THUP
FUMP
TUP
TUP
ZOINK
NO WHISTLE! THAT WAS ALL BALL!
GU...
THROB
OUCH ...
VOOSH

SHIVER
DIS
JOSUI
HIBA

MASATO!
YOU OKAY?
OH, THE PAIN!
HEY, WE NEED SOME ICE! FIRST-AID KIT!
MA-SATO!
I'VE GOT IT.
NO MATTER HOW WE ATTACK THEIR OFFENSE, IT WON'T WORK.
UNLESS NO. 9 IS CRUSHED, WE CAN'T BEAT JOSUI.
YOU'VE ...

... SPRAINED YOUR ANKLE, LOOKS LIKE. I THINK YOU'RE DONE.
NO WAY! I'M OKAY. I CAN PLAY!
ARE YOU SURE?
OUCH.
I QUIT! I QUIT!
BWA HA HA HA
PUSH
WHAT A FACIAL! TAKEN DOWN BY GIRLY BOY!
IF I WERE IN THERE, IT WOULD BE DIFFERENT.
I'M A "TAKE-CHARGE" KIND OF ...
SANTA, GET IN THERE.
WHAT?
ME?
YUP.
IT'S A GOOD GAME.

JOSUI IS VARYING THEIR ATTACKS AND HIBA IS BLOCKING ALL OF THEM.
NO. 4 IS ESPECIALLY TOUGH.
HE HAS SPEED, SKILL, COMPOSURE AND AN EYE FOR THE FLOW OF THE GAME. HE'S A COMPLETE PLAYER.
IT MAKES UP FOR HIS LACK OF SIZE.
IT SEEMS LIKE HE CAN PLAY ANY POSITION. I WONDER WHY HE'S PLAYING DEFENSE.
YOU'VE GOT IT WRONG, SEIJI.
HE'S NOT JUST PLAYING DEFENSE.
HE'S READING JOSUI'S OFFENSE AND DEFENSE, THEN DIRECTING THE GAME.
HE'S MORE LIKE A FIELD GENERAL ...

YOU TWO SHOULD JOIN THE HIBA JUNIOR HIGH **BOOSTER CLUB.** I PERSONALLY THINK JOSUI IS DOING PRETTY WELL.
WHAT ARE YOU GETTING UPSET FOR?
HEH
THE FACT THAT A DEFENDER IS SHOWING SOME GOOD MOVES ONLY MEANS THAT THE OFFENSE IS JUST AS GOOD. HE'S BEING PRESSURED.
ESPECIALLY AFTER THAT CORNER KICK.
HIBA CENTERED TO NO. 4, WHO WASN'T PART OF THE OFFENSE.
NO ONE ANTICIPATED THAT, AND IT WOULD HAVE BEEN A SURPRISE HAD HE SCORED... BUT SHŌ STOPPED HIM.
IT'S PROBABLY NOT THAT SHŌ READ THE PLAY--I THINK HE KEYED ON NO. 4, BECAUSE HE SENSED THE DEFENDER WAS A THREAT.
I BET THAT WAS THE CASE. WATCHING FROM OUT-SIDE THE GAME, IT MAKES SENSE.
I MEAN, SHŌ HAS A SPECIAL KIND OF COMPOSURE... I GET THE FEELING THAT HE CAN MAKE THINGS HAPPEN WHILE HE'S IN THE GAME.

READ THIS WAY
SO YOU HAVE TSUBASA SHIINA, WHO DIRECTS HIS TEAM LIKE A PUPPET MASTER, THROUGH FORCE OF WILL...
...AND SHŌ KAZAMATSURI, WHO FIRES UP HIS TEAM BY PLAYING WITH HEART AND NEVER GIVING UP.
IT'S GONNA BE A BUMPY RIDE.
SUB-STITUTION. NO. 12 IS GOING IN FOR NO. 15.
THUMPA
GULP
THUMPA
THUMPA
SUI

WE'RE COUNTING ON YOU, SANTA!
THUMPA
THUMPA
THUMPA
NOT GOOD. I'M HAVING KITTENS!!
I'VE NEVER PLAYED IN AN ACTUAL GAME BEFORE. I WAS IN LITTLE LEAGUE LIKE A MILLION YEARS AGO, BUT I'VE ONLY REALLY PLAYED IN PRACTICE.
GO GET 'EM!
SHOVE
YIKE
TEETER
GULP
STAGE.92
First Score

STAGE.92
First Score

JOSUI
HIBA
FIRST HALF
SECOND HALF
TOTAL
THAT'S THE HALF!
GOOD GAME, HUH?
SEEMS LIKE IT'S ANYBODY'S GAME.
THEY'RE KEEPING EACH OTHER IN CHECK, BUT THE FLOW OF THE GAME MIGHT CHANGE IN THE SECOND HALF.
I AGREE.
CHATTER
CHATTER
JOSUI

HEY, SANTA!
WHAT'RE YOU DOING? YOU WERE JUST STANDING AROUND DURING THE FIRST HALF!
YOU'VE GOT TO GET AGGRESSIVE!
KNO... KNOCK IT OFF.
YUKI, WHERE'S THE DRINK POWDER ?!
IT'S RIGHT UNDER THERE ...
LIKE I NEED YOU TO TELL ME THAT.
THERE'S A BIG DIFFERENCE BETWEEN WATCHING AND ACTUALLY PLAYING.
EVEN IF I ATTACK THE BALL, THE GAME DEVELOPS SO FAST, I CAN'T KEEP UP. IT WASN'T SUPPOSED TO BE LIKE THIS.

...
SOMETHING WRONG, SHIGEKI?
HMM.
HUH?
HOW ABOUT YOU? YOU SEEM TO BE KICKING BUTT TODAY.
I'M COUNTING ON YOU, BOSS.
STOP CALLING ME "BOSS."

SHI-GEKI.
FLING
!
SW
AP
WHAT'S WITH YOUR RIGHT ARM?
TATSU-BOY!
I DON'T KICK THE BALL WITH MY ARM, DO I?
I'M ENJOYING THE GAME. LET'S JUST PLAY.

JUST DON'T BE RECKLESS, ALL RIGHT?
SHEESH.
CAN'T GUARANTEE IT.
RECK-LESSNESS IS MY SPECIALTY.
TSU-BASA.
C'MON!
PLEASE SHIFT ME OVER...
...TO RIGHT WING.
HIBA

NOPE.
NOPE? BUT...
...
I KNOW YOU HAVE SOME ISSUES WITH NO. 11 ...
...SO I INTENTIONALLY MOVED YOU TO THE LEFT.
I UNDER-STAND THAT YOU WANT TO TAKE HIM ON.
BUT HE WOULD TOTALLY SCHOOL YOU.
SIZZLE
GRIP

TSU-BASA, I WANT TO SWITCH, TOO.
IT'S EASIER FOR ME TO PLAY THE LEFT SIDE.
MA-SAKI.
EVEN IF IT'S A MIS-MATCH, IT'S OKAY, ISN'T IT?
ALL WE HAVE TO DO IS TO MAKE SURE WE COVER THAT SIDE.
GEEZ.
OKAY, OKAY.
DURING THE SECOND HALF, MASAKI WILL TAKE LEFT WING, AND NAOKI WILL TAKE RIGHT.
ALL RIGHT!!
BUT, IN EXCHANGE ...
HIBA

...YOU'D BETTER SHOW ME YOUR BEST STUFF.
JOLT
DON'T YOU *DARE* DISAPPOINT ME.
OKAY!
ALSO ...
...I FIGURED OUT HOW WE CAN BREAK DOWN JOSUI.
IT'S TIME. LET'S GO GET SOME GOALS.

SECOND HALF. EVERYBODY FOCUS!
YEAH!
KAORU.
YEAH?
FEED SANTA THE BALL. HE NEEDS TO SHAKE OFF THE RUST.
SURE, COACH.
TWEE

TUMP
THUMPA
SANTA!
FUMP
VOOSH
AH!
BOMP
JOSUI

SANTA! IN FRONT!
WHAT?
JOSUI

DURING THE FIRST HALF, NO. 15 DIDN'T TOUCH THE BALL AT ALL. SO, I BET THEY'LL GIVE THE BALL TO HIM AT THE START OF THE SECOND HALF.
WHEN THEY DO, TAKE HIM DOWN.
AH.
GOT IT!
JOSUI
HIBA
JOSUI
WHOOSH

SMAP
OH NO!
TOO

BAMP
WISSH
GOAL!!

I CAN'T BELIEVE IT!
STRAIGHT AWAY...
TAKING ADVANTAGE OF THE NERVOUS SUB ON HIS FIRST TOUCH.
THAT'S JUST WHAT I EXPECTED FROM HIBA.
IT WAS MY FAULT.
MY ADVICE BACK-FIRED.
S... SORRY.
I... I...
YO, OCTOPUS!
SMAP
TRAPPING A PASS IS THE MOST BASIC OF BASICS, YOU KNOW.
WHAT HAPPENED TO YOUR FUNDA-MENTALS...? GET A GRIP.
I'M SORRY.
IT WAS PARTIALLY OUR FAULT, TOO.
JOSU

HE'S BEEN ON THE RESERVE LIST FOR A LONG TIME, AND HE'S JUST NOW GETTING PLAYING TIME. NO WONDER HE'S NERVOUS.
IF ONLY WE'D LET HIM TOUCH THE BALL IMMEDIATELY AFTER HE CAME IN, HE WOULDN'T HAVE BEEN SO STIFF.
NOW THAT HIS MISTAKE ALLOWED THEM TO SCORE, HE'S EVEN MORE MESSED UP.
DON'T WORRY, SANTA.
WE'VE STILL GOT A LOT OF TIME TO TURN THINGS AROUND.
WE'D BETTER DO SOME-THING ABOUT HIM.
TATSUYA, CAN I HAVE A QUICK WORD?
HM?
JOSUI, KICKS OFF.
TWEE
FOOMP
!
BIP

ZUP
SANTA, PASS!
BEAM
SIZZLE
WHAT THE...? ARE YOU MAKING FUN OF ME?!
YOU DON'T HAVE TO COME UP AND KISS ME...
YOU'RE DISSING ME!
VUMP

ANOTHER ONE!
FUMP
DON'T BE RIDICULOUS!
BOOMP
I'M NOT BEING RIDICULOUS.
ANOTHER.
FUMP
...
WHAT THE HECK?
WHAT IS SHŌ DOING?
FUP
FUP
FFUP

WHY ARE YOU LETTING THEM THROUGH ?!
THEY'RE ATTACKING!
AH!
HIBA
BOOMP
FOOM
THUP

FWAAP
JOLT
...
ZOINK
CLOSE ONE!
SHŌ ...
LET'S KEEP IT UP.
GLOW
MAYBE HE IS A GOOD GUY.
PAT
NICE PASS.

WHISTLE!

STAGE.93
Off in the Distance

DASH
SANTA, CROSS IT!

GOOD JOB, SANTA.
TUP
SHOOM
FOOM
TOUCH PASS! THEY'VE BROKEN THROUGH ...
THOOM

VOOO
SH
DON'T EVEN THINK ABOUT IT...
... SHIGEKI!
MONKEY!
JOSUI

HE WILL TOTALLY SCHOOL YOU...
I KNOW HE'S BETTER THAN I AM.
TSUBASA...
BUT THIS FIGHT IS SOMETHING...
...I CAN'T LOSE. *NO MATTER WHAT.*
BRING IT ON, SHIGEKI!
SHI-GEKI.
NA-OKI.

TODAY, I'LL FORCE YOU...
....TO SHOW ME SOME RESPECT!
THWOOP
STOMP
THIS IS IT!

ROLLING THE BALL UNDER HIS LEFT FOOT, HE FEINTS TO THE LEFT ONCE.
THEN, HE FAKES A KICK TO THE RIGHT AS HE STEPS OVER IT.
THEN HE'LL MOVE TO THE LEFT. THAT'S THE MOVE!
WOOSH
HE STEPPED OVER IT.
IT'S THE LEFT!!

WHAT?
VOOM
SHOOM

HOW DID...?
GAHH!
IT'S NOT LIKE I LOST!
IT'S JUST THAT I HAPPENED TO BE A LITTLE TIRED TODAY!
YOU ALWAYS "HAPPEN" TO BE SOMETHING OR ANOTHER.
WE'LL GO AGAIN TOMORROW.
I WON'T LOSE!
TOMORROW?
WHAT? DOESN'T THAT WORK FOR YOU?
HM.

TOMORROW THEN.
BUT THE FOLLOWING DAY...
...HE DIDN'T SHOW UP.
GEEZ!
THAT MORON!
HAVE YOU HEARD?
I HEARD THAT SATŌ'S BOY...RAN AWAY FROM HOME YESTERDAY.
ISN'T SATŌ THE MISTRESS OF THAT RICH MERCHANT, FUJIMURA?
SO THAT STORY IS TRUE...
GOSSIP
GOSSIP

I MEAN, THE STORY ABOUT HAVING THE MISTRESS'S CHILD MADE THE HEIR OF THE FUJIMURA FORTUNE. AFTER ALL, THEY'VE HAD ALL GIRLS IN THAT FAMILY.
I HEAR SATŌ IS GETTING RE-MARRIED TOO.
WHEN THE BOY WAS BORN, HE WAS NOT ACKNOWLEDGED BY HIS FATHER. AND NOW HIS MOTHER IS GOING TO THROW HIM OUT.
I FEEL SO SORRY FOR THAT BOY...
HOW COME ?!
HOW COME DIDN'T HE SAY ANYTHING ABOUT THAT?
IT'S AS IF HE WAS A STRANGER.
YOU WERE ALWAYS LIKE THAT. EVEN WHEN I FACE YOU STRAIGHT ON, YOU SKIP AROUND ME.
YOU RUN AWAY WITHOUT SAYING ANYTHING IMPORTANT.
THAT'S WHY I ...
SHIGEKI !!

SWAP

NOT TODAY!
I WON'T LET YOU GET AWAY!
PREPARE YOURSELF!!
DASH DASH DASH
THUD
WHAM

TIME FOR YOU TO GET OFF MY BACK!
MONKEY!
SHUT UP!
ADMIT DEFEAT. THIS IS A LONG TIME COMING, SHIGEKI!
NEVER!
THUD
TRIP
THUP
STOMP

DA
!
A
A
SH
GOT HIM WITH THE PULL-PUSH?!
THAT GUY HAS AMAZING BALANCE!
I...
I WON'T LET YOU GET AWAY!
SK
KRRRP

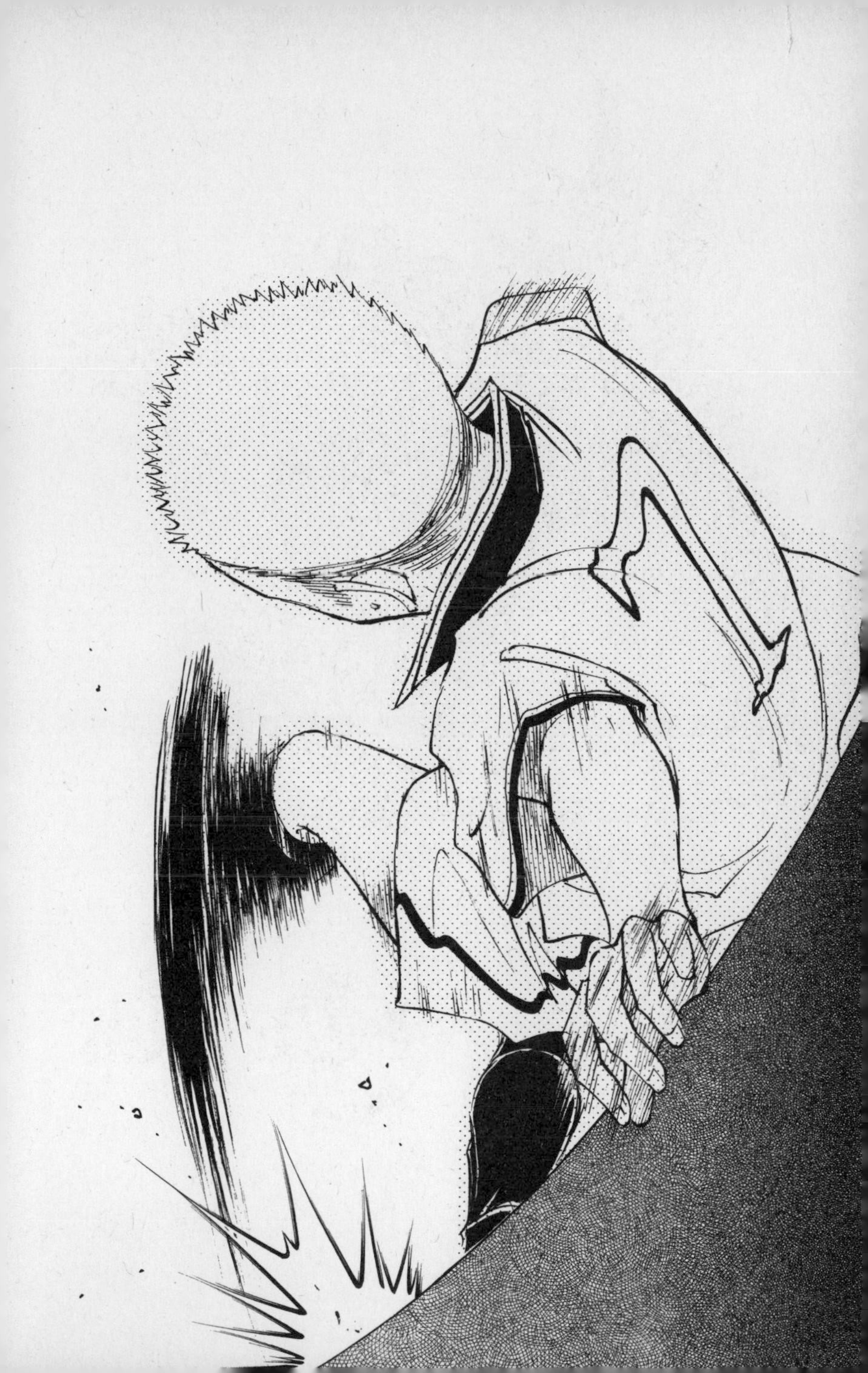

NO!
SO THAT'S THE WAY IT'S GONNA BE?

HAVE IT YOUR WAY!
SHIGEKI!

ZUP
BAM
THE LAST PASS FROM NO. 11 IS CUT OFF BY A HIBA DEFENDER!
...BUT A WONDERFUL PLAY.
BUP
NO GOAL...
HUFF

WHAT'S WRONG?
YOU LOOK GLUM.
LEAVE ME ALONE.
OKAY ...
GONNA LAY DOWN AND QUIT NOW THAT I'VE BEATEN YOU?
TWITCH
SHUT UP!
NOBODY'S GOTTEN BEAT JUST YET! WE'RE JUST GETTING STARTED!
VOOP
HIBA

WAY TO GET FIRED UP...
BEAM
... NAOKI.
ARE YOU OKAY, NAOKI?
?
HE'S A NASTY PIECE OF WORK...
HE REMEMBERED MY NAME AFTER ALL.
IT'S NOTHING.
THE REAL GAME IS ABOUT TO BEGIN!

STAGE.94 The Tying Goal

WE'RE GONNA DESTROY THEM!
YEAH!

FOOOM
VOOOSH
AH.
HIBA
AFTER HE INTERCEPTED THE BALL...
...HE SENT THE LONG BALL DOWNFIELD!
THOOM
IT'S A SWIFT ATTACK!!
HIBA IS CHALLENGING AGAIN!!

CENTER-
ING!
NOOO!

THREE OF THEM ARE ATTACKING THE GOAL ?!
HIBA
HE BARELY STOPPED IT.
HIBA STILL HAS THE BALL.
FWAM
THE KEEPER JUMPED SIDEWAYS!

SMAAP
NO. 8 CLEARS!
BOOOM
BUT HIBA PUSHES BACK!
AHH!

SWAAP
ONCE AGAIN, NO. 8 CLEARS!
I WON'T MAKE THE SAME MISTAKE TWICE!
GET...

FWAP
...OUTTA
MY FACE!

FWAAM
ZOOP
STRIKERS! ATTACK!!

THEY REPELLED HIBA'S FURIOUS ATTACK ...
...AND NOW IT'S JOSUI'S TURN.
VOOOM

BOOMP
DASH

TRAPPING THE BALL ...
SWAP
SNAP

SPIN
TUMP
BUMP
WHAT?

THE OFFSIDE TRAP FAILED!
NO. 10 IS FREE! THE KEEPER IS CHARGING HIM!!
HE DODGED IT!
GOT IT!
FOOOSH
BOOM
TOSUI

SWAP
FORGET ABOUT IT!
HMPH!

GLANCE
THIS TIME, IT'S JOSUI WITH THE FIERCE ATTACK!
BUT HIBA STUCK TO ITS GUNS!
JOSUI CANNOT SCORE!
TICK

ONE GOAL...

PLEASE ...
IT'S NOT LOOKING GOOD...
HEY.
THIS IS BORING...
WHY CAN'T THEY SCORE WHEN THEY'RE ATTACKING SO MUCH?
...
WHY?
IT LOOKS LIKE WE'LL LOSE.
STOP IT!
CAN'T YOU SEE THEY'RE TRYING ?!
C'MON, IT'S THE *TRUTH*, RIGHT?
SO ARE YOU GOING TO STOP ROOTING FOR THEM?

THEY'RE ALL DOING THEIR BEST. GOING BEYOND EVEN WHAT I TAUGHT THEM.
BUT THEY STILL CAN'T SCORE.
THEY'RE GETTING EXHAUSTED.
AT THIS POINT, IT'S A BATTLE OF WILLS.
AND IT'LL ALL BE OVER THE MOMENT THEY GIVE UP.

FOOM
WHAM
YOU...
THROB
UNNHH...
YANK
YER NOT GOING ANYWHERE!

HIBA
BOMP
HIBA
JOSUI
WHAT?!

BOOM
HIBA
GOAL!
YES!

STAGE.95 Decision
FOOOSH
GOAL!
WE DID IT!

WAIT...
WE'RE 25 MINUTES INTO THE SECOND HALF, AND IT'S TIED 1-1!
FINALLY, JOSUI GETS THE EQUALIZER!

THAT GUY ...
...HE PULLED ONE OVER ON ME!
IT'S STILL ANYBODY'S GAME!
HAND BALL!
THAT PLAY...

NO GOAL!
HMPH!
HE SAW IT, HUH?
HUH? WHAT?
HOW COME IT'S NO GOAL?
DIDN'T HE JUST SCORE?
WHAT'S UP, MATSU-SHITA?
THE LINESMAN SAW IT ...
WE'RE SAVED.
PHEW!

I KNEW IT.
WHEN HE TRAPPED THE BALL BEHIND HIS BACK, IT TOUCHED HIS HAND.
IT WAS THE REF'S BLIND SPOT, BUT I COULD SEE IT FROM MY SIDE.
BUT THAT WAS...
SHIGEKI.

WAS THAT...
ER...
OR... DID YOUR HAND JUST BUMP THE BALL?
...WAS IT DELIBERATE?
...
WHAT IF IT **WAS** DELIBERATE?
WHAT'RE YOU GONNA DO ABOUT IT?
!
SHIG...
SHŌ, DO YOU WANT TO DO WHAT IT TAKES TO WIN THIS GAME, OR WHAT?
WELL?
I...
I...

STAGE.95
Decision

FOOM
HIBA TAKES THE FREE KICK.
THERE'S ONLY A LITTLE TIME LEFT.
WHAT IF IT WAS DELIBERATE?
THAT LAST CALL REALLY PUTS THE HURT ON JOSUI!
DO YOU WANT TO DO WHAT IT TAKES TO WIN THIS GAME, OR WHAT?
OR WHAT?
OR WHAT?

READ THIS WAY
AH.
VUMP
DAAH!
WHAT'S HE DOING?!
HE LOST HIS FOCUS? AND THERE'S NO TIME LEFT...
WHAT'S WRONG, SHŌ?!
WHAT'S WRONG WITH SHŌ?
A MISSED OPPORTUNITY.
I BET...
...HE CAN'T MAKE UP HIS MIND.

CAN'T MAKE UP HIS MIND?
LET'S SAY, SEIJI...
ABOUT WHAT?
...IN A SITUATION JUST LIKE THIS...
...IF YOU DIDN'T GET A HAND BALL AND GOT THE GOAL, HOW WOULD YOU FEEL?
LUCKY! ♡
SLUMP
IDIOT...
GUESS I SHOULDN'T HAVE ASKED YOU THAT.
HEY, THAT'S NOT COOL.
C'MON, CAP. DON'T END IT LIKE THAT.
WELL...
SHŌ PROBABLY WOULDN'T FEEL HAPPY LIKE YOU WOULD, EVEN IF THEY GOT THE GOAL.
AHEM
IT'S FINE IF THE REF SAYS IT'S OKAY, RIGHT?
THAT'S ALSO A TECHNIQUE, AFTER ALL.
THAT'S RIGHT. IF ONE GOAL IS ALL THAT MATTERS...
...THEY SHOULD BE RUTHLESS ABOUT GETTING IT.

READ THIS WAY

SHOOM
THREE MINUTES LEFT!
CLASH
JUST TRY IT!
SNEER

FWAP
HE'S GOOD!
NUT-MEGGED HIM!
PIECE OF CAKE.
BURN
NO WAY!
HE'S PAST ONE!
DASH
TWIST
NO. 4 IS RUSHING TO COVER THE GOAL.

NO. 11 IS SAND-WICHED!
VOO
SH
BUT NO. 11 ...
... WON'T GIVE UP!
HE'S TENACIOUS !!
THERE ARE TWO OF YOU, AND YOU CAN'T EVEN STRIP THE BALL.
YOU GUYS ARE **WEAK.**
WHAT ?!
RAGE

FLICK
!?
FUMP
WOW!
HE INTENTIONALLY KICKED THE BALL INTO THE DEFENDER'S BODY...
DASH
TUMP
...AND MOVED THE BALL INTO THE OPEN?!
YOU!
GO-SUKE!

STOP!
DON'T TAKE THE BAIT!!
WHOA.
JERK
WHAT?
WUMP
OH, NO...
TWEEE

FOUL! HE TOOK OUT NO. 11'S FOOT.
PENALTY KICK!
HE DID IT!
WAY TO GO, SHIGEKI!
AT THE ELEVENTH HOUR, JOSUI GETS A CHANCE.
PAT
HOP
THANKS FOR THE GIFT.
JUST RETURNING THE FAVOR.
YOU PUNK! CHEATER!
HEY, STOP.
JOSUI

JOSUI
COME TO THINK OF IT...
...YOU HAVEN'T ANSWERED MY QUESTION, SHŌ.

THIS PENALTY ...
...IS YOUR KICK.
SHI-GEKI!
I CAN'T! I CAN'T DO THAT ...
YOU CAN'T KICK A PENALTY FROM A GIFT CALL?
I CAN'T MOVE SO WELL. MY SHOULDER HURTS.
TOSU

THIS KICK...
...WILL GIVE ME YOUR ANSWER.
SHOOM

THUMPA
WE'RE COUNTING ON YOU, SHŌ!
SLAM IT IN!
THUMPA
HUFF
I JUST DON'T KNOW...
THUMPA
SHŌ ...
WHAT SHOULD I DO...?
THUMPA

JOSUI
JOSUI
WHAT...
WHAT KIND OF SOCCER DO I WANT TO PLAY?
JOSUI

STAGE.96
I'm Going to Win

WHAT'S
IT GONNA
BE?

READ THIS WAY
DO YOU WANT TO DO WHAT IT TAKES TO WIN THIS GAME, OR WHAT?
HOW ABOUT IT, SHŌ?
GASP
HUFF
GASP
THUMPA
I...
HUFF
THUMPA
I...

GULP
THE PENALTY IS A TOUGH BREAK FOR US. ONLY ABOUT TWO OR THREE MINUTES LEFT.
IT'LL BE HARD TO GET THIS BACK. DANG! IT'S GOING TO BE AN EXTENDED GAME, HUH?

EVERY-
ONE.

I'M SORRY.

HIBA
9

WHAT?!
A BIG MISS. DID THE PRESSURE GET TO HIM?
THE KICK IS NO GOOD!!
I KNEW IT.
SO, THAT'S YOUR ANSWER, HUH?
YOU DON'T WANNA PLAY SOCCER WITH WINNERS AND LOSERS...
YOU WANT A TOUCHY-FEELY GAME WITH GOOD FRIENDS. I GET IT.
THAT FOOL.

WHAT'RE YOU DOING, SHŌ?!
IT WAS A GREAT OPPORTUNITY TO TIE!!
IF I KICKED ...
MASATO!
WUMP
...
THROB
GAAH!
FUMB
IT'S NO USE.
WE CAN'T WIN.
HMM...

HE REALLY IS STRAIGHT-LACED.
HE'S CHOSEN A DIFFICULT PATH.
YOU KNOW WHAT YOU'VE DONE, RIGHT?
YOU'LL HAVE TO CLEAN UP THE MESS ON YOUR OWN.
YES.
IT...
IT COULDN'T HAVE BEEN HELPED!
HE'S ONLY HUMAN. PEOPLE MAKE MISTAKES!
HE WAS UNDER INCREDIBLE PRESSURE NOT TO FAIL! IT WOULD BE WEIRD IF HE WASN'T NERVOUS...
IT'S OKAY, YŪSUKE.

SHŌ?
I KNOW IT WAS SELFISH.
BUT I JUST COULDN'T DO IT.
I'M SORRY.
YOU MEAN ...
...YOU *INTENTIONALLY* MISSED? IS THAT IT?
...
NOD
WHAT'S THAT SUPPOSED TO MEAN?
WHAT'RE YOU THINKING?
WHY DID YOU DO THAT?
PLEASE EXPLAIN YOURSELF.
TWEE TWEE TWEE

TAKE YOUR POSITIONS, SO WE CAN START!
WHAT ARE YOU DOING?
SLUMP
SLUMP
EVERY-BODY! MOVE!
WE STILL HAVE TIME. LET'S GO FOR THE TIE, AND GET INTO EXTENDED TIME.
SORRY.
TOSUI
THIS WILL COST YOU. WHAT'RE YOU GOING TO DO, SHŌ?
IT WASN'T JUST THE LOST GOAL.
YOU LET THEM LOSE FAITH IN YOU.

READ THIS WAY
I NEED TO THINK OF THE TEAM'S VICTORY, NOT MY PERSONAL CONCERNS.
SO, WHY DID I...?
WHAT A STUBBORN LITTLE BUGGER YOU ARE. YOU'D RATHER PLAY IT CLEAN THAN WIN, HUH?
I DON'T WANT TO LOSE.
HOW'S THAT?
IF I WENT FOR THE PENALTY OR TRIED TO GET A FOUL, IT WOULD BE LIKE ADMITTING THAT WE CAN'T BEAT HIBA IN A FAIR FIGHT. I COULDN'T STAND IT.
SHEESH, THIS GUY ...
I HAVEN'T GIVEN UP, YET.

THIS IS ONE GAME...
...I'M GOING TO WIN!
JOSUI

WHOOP-DEE-DO! SO THE LITTLE BOY SCOUT REALLY HATES TO LOSE! THIS SHOULD BE FUN.
YOU PUFFED-UP LITTLE PUNK!
WE'VE GOT THREE MINUTES LEFT, AND YOU'RE SAYING YOU'LL SCORE TWO GOALS AGAINST *THAT DEFENSE?*
YOU'VE GOT A HIGH OPINION OF YOURSELF, SUPERSTAR! GO AHEAD AND TRY IT. I'LL VISIT YOU AT THE HOSPITAL.
I THOUGHT IT WAS GOING TO BE INTER-ESTING.
HOW DIS-APPOINTING.
IT LOOKS LIKE I OVERRATED NO. 9.
OH WELL. THIS ONE'S IN THE BAG.

THE GAME'S OVER.
THEY HAD GOOD TEAMWORK UP TO NOW, BUT ...
...BLOWING THE PENALTY TOOK THE WIND OUT OF THEIR SAILS.
SHŌ'S SO PATHETIC. I THOUGHT HE MIGHT BE COOL, BUT HE WASN'T THAT GREAT AFTER ALL.
WE'VE LOST THIS GAME.
I DON'T UNDER-STAND.
HE INTEN-TIONALLY MISSED THE TARGET? DOES SHŌ WANT TO LOSE?
MUTTER
MUTTER
NO, THAT CANNOT BE THE CASE. BASED ON THE EVIDENCE ...
MUTTER
IT DOESN'T MAKE SENSE. SHŌ'S THINKING IS *ILLOGICAL.*
WILL YOU *STOP IT?!*

READ THIS WAY

BUT I HAVE A FEELING IT WON'T END LIKE THIS.
AS A KEEPER, I CAN SENSE THE POSSIBILITIES....
KŌ, LIKE YOU SAID, IF SHŌ MISSED THE TARGET ON PURPOSE, DON'T YOU THINK THE SITUATION'S PRETTY BAD?
HE'S ALL ALONE OUT THERE.
HE MIGHT HAVE EVEN TURNED HIS TEAMMATES INTO ENEMIES.
HE'S TOO HONEST FOR HIS OWN GOOD. THERE'RE EASIER WAYS TO GO ABOUT DOING THINGS...
...BUT HE ALWAYS DIVES IN HEAD-FIRST.
THEN AGAIN, I'VE NEVER SEEN HIM FAIL AT SOME-THING...
...AFTER HE'S MADE UP HIS MIND TO DO IT.

READ THIS WAY

WHISTLE!

STAGE.97
RUN

AFTER HE MISSED THE PENALTY KICK...
...JOSUI STARTED SHOWING CRACKS IN ITS TEAMWORK.
HESITATION, ANXIETY AND LOST FAITH...
THERE'S HARDLY ANY TIME LEFT IN THE SECOND HALF. THEY'RE ALREADY OUT OF GAS...
...AND NOW THEY'RE PSYCHED OUT, TOO.
JOSUI
I HAD A FEELING THERE WAS SOMETHING MORE TO THAT KID, BUT...
...IT'S TOO BAD.

GLANCE
WE HAVE NO TIME!
HALT
BREAK THROUGH THE FLAT THREE?
IMPOSSIBLE.
FOOM
DO IT, SHŌ!!

FOOOM
LUNGE
!?
HALT

HUH?!
NO. 11 DIDN'T REACT TO THE PASS?!
FOOOOM

IS IT A MIS-COMMUNICATION? THE PASS SEEMED TO GO TO NO ONE IN PARTICULAR...
ROKUSUKE, BEHIND YOU!
ARGH!
VOOOM
NO. 11 WAS A DECOY!!

WHAT?
PROVE ME WRONG, SHŌ.
WAIT!
NO. 9 IS ATTACKING! BUT...CAN HE RUN DOWN THE PASS?
SHOW US YOU CAN DO IT!

SHŌ!!

NO. 9 HAS PLAYED HARD FOR TWO FULL HALVES.
IT'S STUPID TO EXPECT HIM TO CATCH THAT PASS.
THAT'S TOUGH...
NO. 4 IS CLOSING ON HIM!
SHŌ.
SHŌ...
PLEASE MAKE IT!
NO WAY...

DASH
DASH
JOSUI
HIBA
DASH
HIBA
GASP
GASP
CREAK
CREAK

LUNGE
CLATTER

AH!
FUMP

READ THIS WAY

GOAL.

GOAL!
ARGH!

THOOOM

CLANG
WHOOF

GOAL!
RAAHH
HE SCORED FROM AN IMPOSSIBLE ANGLE!
SHIOMI.
KENSUKE SHIOMI.

WHAT ?!
GRRR
HE...
...SURPRISES ME SOMETIMES.
TOSUI
TOSUI

WE'RE STILL ONLY TIED.
MAYBE HE'S AN EXTRAORDINARY DUDE.
YUP.
IT'S A NEW GAME!
STAY FOCUSED!
WE CAN DO IT!
LET'S TURN THE TABLES ON HIBA!

WHISTLE!

STAGE.98 The Winning Goal

THIS ONE PLAY WILL DETERMINE IT.
FOOM
IT'S LIKE A STREET FIGHT IN FRONT OF THE GOAL!
LEMME IN THERE!

CURVE
SHOVE
I...
OOPS.
TWIST
NO. 9 IS BLOCKED OUT OF THE PLAY BY NO. 4!

AHH!
CRASH!

FWAM
ROKU-SUKE!
HE TRIED FOR THE HEADER!
THE BALL IS STILL IN PLAY!
THUD
!
!
BUP
THE BALL IS ROLLING TOWARD THE GOAL!

SHWAP
C...
CLEARED !!
OUCH.
JERK
HIBA
JOSUI

THUMP
GAK!
THOOF

AH...
G... GOAL!
TWEE TWEE TWEE
UNBELIEVEBLE!
THE CLEARED BALL HIT THE HEAD OF A JOSUI PLAYER WHO HAD FALLEN DOWN.

THAT'S THE GAME.
HIBA JUNIOR HIGH IS IN COMPLETE SHOCK!
THEIR TOUGH DEFENSE SIMPLY RAN OUT OF LUCK.
HIBA
...
WE WON?
TOSUI
THROB
STAGGER
DON'T MOVE!
TOSUI
WHO DIDDIT? WHO STOMPED ON ME?!
JOLT
YOU OKAY?
WHO'DA THOUGHT SANTA WOULD SAVE US?
HM? WHERE IS SANTA?
AH, HERE'S MIYUKI.
WHAT ?!
SPIN

THUMP
HOW'S YOUR HEAD, SANTA?
JUST PART OF THE JOB, BABY.
YOU WERE INCRED-IBLE! ♡
DAZE DAZE
WHOOSH
OH, YOU THINK SO, MIYUKI?
POOR SHŌ!

HOW'S YOUR HEAD?
OH NO! YOU'RE BLEEDING !!
THANKS.
OH, IT'S NOTHING. ♡
HEY, YOU STILL ALIVE?
POKE POKE
LINE UP, QUICKLY! OTHERWISE, WE CAN'T FINISH THE GAME!
JOLT
WHAT'S YOUR NAME?
NO. 9.

I'M TSUBASA SHIINA.
SHŌ KAZAMA-TSURI.
TODAY, WE JUST HAD BAD LUCK. THAT'S ALL.
OUR FIGHT ISN'T SETTLED YET, OKAY?
NOPE.
IT'S OVER!
JOSUI WINS 2 TO 1.
I'M STILL TALLER THAN YOU.
SMAK
SMAK
OUCH.
HIBA

READ THIS WAY
SOB!
BIG BRO!
WHAT THE? DON'T CRY, YOU MORON!
PAT
FLOP
!
UNCALLED FOR, JERK.
OKAY, OKAY.
THANKS.
ARE YOU CRYING?
SHUDDUP. IT'S JUST A RUNNY NOSE.

WILL YOU STOP SCREWING AROUND? IT'S GOOD WE WON, BUT YOU GOTTA REMEMBER IT'S A TOURNAMENT MATCH.
YOU'D BETTER THINK ABOUT YOUR TEAMMATES MORE.
C'MON, TAKE IT EASY.
YOU'RE BEING PRETTY RECKLESS WITH YOURSELF.
SQUEEZE
...
THE STATE YOU'RE IN, I BET IT WAS DIFFICULT JUST TO RUN.
IT'S OKAY TO TOUGH IT OUT, BUT GET THAT LOOKED AT.
YOU'D PREFER TO SHOW UP HIBA WITH YOUR BRILLIANT MOVES, BUT ALL YOU COULD MANAGE WITH YOUR BUM ARM WERE A FEW CONVINCING FLOPS.
ADMITTING YOU'RE IN PAIN WILL RUIN YOUR IMAGE, YOU KNOW, SHIGEKI.
SHUT YER PIE HOLE, CAPPY!
SHIGEKI.

GOOD STUFF OUT THERE.
JOSUI

SURE.
BUT DON'T EVER TALK BACK TO ME.
EVEN THOUGH YOU'VE BECOME A BETTER PLAYER, YOU AIN'T AT MY LEVEL, YET.
SQUEEZE
THANK YOU VERY MUCH.
GOOD GAME.
WE LEARNED A LOT.
SAME HERE. WE WERE LUCKY.
ER... EXCUSE ME, I'M THE TEACHER IN CHARGE.
TEAMS MAKE THEIR OWN LUCK.
VICTORY CAN BE SNATCHED AWAY IN A HEARTBEAT.
TSUBASA LEARNED THAT TODAY. IT'S A HARD LESSON.

READ THIS WAY

...I SAW THE GHOST OF KENSUKE SHIOMI IN NO. 9, THE ONE WHO CAUGHT UP TO THE BALL BY THE LINE AND SHOT.
YOU SEE IT, TOO?
HE'S MY FATHER.

11 RUN (The End)

WHISTLE! THEATRE!!

He's a papa, after all.

MANGA BY SEKI, ASSISTANT S

Kansai Peeps

A Team With Character(s)

DAISUKE'S NOTES

NAOKI INOUE

PERSONAL DATA	
BIRTHDAY	MAY 5, 1983
SIZE	5' 5" 125 lbs
BLOOD TYPE	O
FAVORITE FOOD:	BEEF TONGUE, MILKY CANDY
DISLIKES:	COCKROACHES
HOBBY AND SPECIAL SKILLS:	OCTOPUS BALLS (I MAKE MY OWN)

MASAKI KUROKAWA

PERSONAL DATA	
BIRTHDAY	NOV 23, 1984
SIZE	5' 8" 130 lbs
BLOOD TYPE	A
FAVORITE FOOD:	CURRY NOODLES
DISLIKES:	VULGARITY
HOBBY AND SPECIAL SKILLS:	THE OUTDOORS, SWIMMING

TSUBASA SHIINA

PERSONAL DATA	
BIRTHDAY	APRIL 19, 1983
SIZE	4' 11" 95 lbs
BLOOD TYPE	B
FAVORITE FOOD:	ITALIAN GELATO
DISLIKES:	SANCTIMONIOUS JERKS
HOBBY AND SPECIAL SKILLS:	MOVIE MARATHONS, MACHINE-GUN TALKING, SELF-DEFENSE

MIYUKI SAKURAI

PERSONAL DATA	
BIRTHDAY	APRIL 27, 1985
SIZE	4' 11" 81 lbs
BLOOD TYPE	O
FAVORITE FOOD:	STRAWBERRY TARTS
DISLIKES:	GREEN PEPPERS, GARLIC
HOBBY AND SPECIAL SKILLS:	BAKING

MAIKO KAMIJO

PERSONAL DATA	
BIRTHDAY	AUG 29, 1984
SIZE	5' 4" 99 lbs
BLOOD TYPE	B
FAVORITE FOOD:	SUPER-SPICY RICE CRACKERS
DISLIKES:	JAPANESE SWEETS
HOBBY AND SPECIAL SKILLS:	HORSE RIDING, COOKING (BUT DON'T EAT IT)

Next in Whistle!

IN THE DISTANCE

Shô, Tatsuya and Daichi have been invited to try out for an all-star team that will compete on an international level. New and old rivals alike gather to vie for spots on the select team, but for Shô, it's gut-check time when he realizes that his technical skills are on the bottom end of the curve. Will he be able to make the cut?

Available July 2006!

LEGENDZ
Ken and Shiron's friendship faces the ultimate test!
CONCLUDING VOLUME OF THE SERIES!!
ONLY $7.99 EACH!
Vols. 1-4 on sale now!
ON SALE AT:
www.shonenjump.com
Also available at your local bookstore and comic store.
VIZ media
RATED A FOR ALL AGES
SHONEN JUMP MANGA
LEGENDZ © 2003 BY Makoto Haruno, Rin Hirai/SHUEISHA Inc. ©2003 WiZ

LAST SAIYAN STANDING!
DRAGON BALL Z™
On sale now!
DRAGON BALL Z
SHONEN JUMP MANGA
Story & Art by
Akira Toriyama
volume 25
DRAGON BALL Z
SHONEN JUMP GRAPHIC NOVEL
Story & Art by
Akira Toriyama
volume 1
On sale at:
WWW.SHONENJUMP.COM
Also available at your local bookstore and comic store.
DRAGON BALL © 1984 by BIRD STUDIO/SHUEISHA Inc.
RATED T FOR TEEN
viz media
SJ

BEET GETS A THOUGHTFUL BEATING BY A MYSTERIOUS WARRIOR!
Beet™
THE VANDEL BUSTER
ONLY $7.99! AND UNDER
On sale now!
SHONEN JUMP™ MANGA
BOUKEN OH BEET-BEET THE VANDEL BUSTER-
© 2002 by RIKU SANJO, KOJI INADA/SHUEISHA Inc.

ONE PIECE
ONE PIECE
Who'll save Luffy from the bottom of the ocean?
Vols. 1-10 on sale now!
SHONEN JUMP MANGA
ONE PIECE © 1997 by Eiichiro Oda/SHUEISHA Inc.

Intense one-on-one battles reveal a new side of the student ninja!
Also look for Naruto video games coming to the PlayStation®2 soon!
Vols. 1-9 on sale now!
NARUTO
SHONEN JUMP MANGA
Story & Art by Masashi Kishimoto volume 9
NARUTO
Masashi Kishimoto volume 1
ONLY $7.95! EACH
NARUTO™
On sale at:
WWW.SHONENJUMP.COM
Also available at your local bookstore and comic store.
viz media
SJ
RATED T FOR TEEN
NARUTO © 1999 by Masashi Kishimoto/SHUEISHA Inc.